Business Guides on the Go

"Business Guides on the Go" presents cutting-edge insights from practice on particular topics within the fields of business, management, and finance. Written by practitioners and experts in a concise and accessible form the series provides professionals with a general understanding and a first practical approach to latest developments in business strategy, leadership, operations, HR management, innovation and technology management, marketing or digitalization. Students of business administration or management will also benefit from these practical guides for their future occupation/careers.

These Guides suit the needs of today's fast reader.

Reinhard Ematinger • Matthias Renner •
Sandra Schulze

Setting Goals with LEGO® SERIOUS PLAY®

A Proven Approach
for Forward-Thinking Organizations

Reinhard Ematinger 🆔
Maisbach, Germany

Matthias Renner
Frankfurt, Germany

Sandra Schulze
Maisbach, Germany

ISSN 2731-4758　　　　　ISSN 2731-4766　(electronic)
Business Guides on the Go
ISBN 978-3-031-67856-1　　　ISBN 978-3-031-67857-8　(eBook)
https://doi.org/10.1007/978-3-031-67857-8

© The Editor(s) (if applicable) and The Author(s), under exclusive license to Springer Nature Switzerland AG 2024

This work is subject to copyright. All rights are solely and exclusively licensed by the Publisher, whether the whole or part of the material is concerned, specifically the rights of translation, reprinting, reuse of illustrations, recitation, broadcasting, reproduction on microfilms or in any other physical way, and transmission or information storage and retrieval, electronic adaptation, computer software, or by similar or dissimilar methodology now known or hereafter developed.

The use of general descriptive names, registered names, trademarks, service marks, etc. in this publication does not imply, even in the absence of a specific statement, that such names are exempt from the relevant protective laws and regulations and therefore free for general use.

The publisher, the authors and the editors are safe to assume that the advice and information in this book are believed to be true and accurate at the date of publication. Neither the publisher nor the authors or the editors give a warranty, expressed or implied, with respect to the material contained herein or for any errors or omissions that may have been made. The publisher remains neutral with regard to jurisdictional claims in published maps and institutional affiliations.

This Springer imprint is published by the registered company Springer Nature Switzerland AG
The registered company address is: Gewerbestrasse 11, 6330 Cham, Switzerland

If disposing of this product, please recycle the paper.

What You Can Find in this *Business Guide on the Go*

- A proven process for defining objectives and measuring results that works in companies of different sizes and industries
- An intelligent combination of Objectives and Key Results with the activating method of LEGO SERIOUS PLAY
- Examples from four companies, which make both the approach and the practical procedure even more comprehensible

Acknowledgments

The authors would like to thank Simon Dutton for his diligent proofreading and skillful translation from the authors' whacky interpretation of English to proper English. His contributions significantly improved the usability of this book.

About this Book

With this *Business Guide on the Go*, Reinhard Ematinger, Matthias Renner, and Sandra Schulze support you in formulating objectives and agreeing results by suggesting a format that makes Objectives and Key Results tangible. The intelligent combination with LEGO® SERIOUS PLAY® ensures that the important topics are literally put on the table. Actual case studies accompany you through this *Business Guide on the Go*, and useful tips in the "Key Takeaways" sections support you in transferring them to the reality of your organization.

Contents

1	**Why Objectives and Key Results?**	**1**
	1.1 Why Is this Topic Worthwhile?	1
	1.2 Origin and Background	2
	1.3 OKRs and Their Neighborhood	10
	1.4 Cases and Applications	18
	1.5 Key Takeaways	22
	References	23
2	**Why LEGO SERIOUS PLAY?**	**25**
	2.1 Background and Building Blocks	25
	2.2 Your First Steps in 3D	33
	2.3 Cases and Applications	44
	2.4 Key Takeaways	50
	References	51
3	**Target Definition in 3D**	**53**
	3.1 Problems and Solutions	53
	3.2 Agenda at a Glance	55
	3.3 Detailed Agenda (Tables 3.1 and 3.2)	57
	3.4 Cases and Applications	61

3.5 The Takeaways 66
References 67

4 Retrospective in 3D 69
4.1 Problems and Solutions 69
4.2 Agenda at a Glance 71
4.3 Detailed Agenda (Tables 4.1 and 4.2) 72
4.4 Cases and Applications 75
4.5 The Takeaways 79
4.6 Instead of a Summary 80

What You Can Take Away from this *Business Guide on the Go* 81

1

Why Objectives and Key Results?

In this section, the authors invite you to familiarize yourself with the past and present of Objectives and Key Results. You will discover commonalities with neighboring concepts and be able to understand their application in four companies.

1.1 Why Is this Topic Worthwhile?

Do you want to consistently implement your priorities, agree goals for yourself and others in the truest sense of the word, for a manageable period of time, and record how you will achieve them in a way that is transparent to everyone involved?

Do you want to make the big picture easier to understand, make your organization's objectives transparent at all times, make decisions more comprehensible, and involve key people more closely than before in the process of defining objectives?

Do you want to finally make your own contribution and that of others more visible, be heard and give everyone a voice, and significantly broaden the perspective of your organization and your customers, partners, and competitors?

Welcome! The idea of Objectives and Key Results ensures a focus is placed on the topics and activities that have been agreed in the form of objectives and results, and the concept of LEGO SERIOUS PLAY creates a common understanding and promotes the willingness of all those involved to realize the objectives.

Objectives and Key Results work in every company, just like a Swiss Army Knife works in every environment, says John Doerr in his book *Measure What Matters* (Doerr 2018). Neither he nor the authors of this *Business Guide on the Go* are interested in pure doctrine, but rather in capturing the essence of the idea, adapting it, and developing it further.

The book is not a complete work on the history, present, and future of Objectives and Key Results. The authors do not claim to present the implementation of, and daily work with, OKR in a detailed manual. Their aim is to contribute to a meaningful combination of Objectives and Key Results and LEGO SERIOUS PLAY.

Two points are important to the authors:

- LEGO® is a trademark of the LEGO Group. The Minifigure, DUPLO®, and LEGO® SERIOUS PLAY® are registered trademarks of the LEGO Group. The authors are neither sponsored nor supported by the LEGO Group.
- The illustrative icons in Fig. 2.3 depicting the OKR cycle were designed by the creative team of Freepik Company S.L. The authors have permission to use them under the Flaticon Basic Licence.

1.2 Origin and Background

Peter Drucker is undoubtedly one of the grandfathers of the idea of Objectives and Key Results with his concept of Management by Objectives (MBO), which he introduced in the 1950s. The pioneer of modern management theory described a process in which employees and managers define objectives and then agree on what needs to be done to achieve them. In doing so, he laid the groundwork for a shift from Industrial Age *management by control* to *management by trust*—arguably the first management philosophy of the dawning information age.

George Doran's work "There is a S.M.A.R.T. way to write management's goals and objectives," published in 1981, built on the work of Edwin Locke (Doran 1981). At the end of the 1960s, the psychologist Locke explained in a scientific paper how setting smart goals increases the results and performance of companies (Locke 1968). George Doran's definition of S.M.A.R.T. as a useful way of formulating goals stands for **s**pecific, **m**easurable, **a**ttractive, **r**ealistic, and **t**ime-bound. Building blocks of this, focusing mainly on results, their timing, and planning, can be found in the concept of Objectives and Key Results.

The term "Objectives and Key Results" was coined by the later Intel CEO Andy Grove, who in the mid-1970s took the idea of Management by Objectives and developed an approach to ensure that Intel focused on its objectives, defined results, and tracked them regularly. At the time, Intel was undergoing a transformation from a memory chip manufacturer to a microprocessor supplier, and management wanted to ensure that employees were focused on the goals that would make this transformation possible. Andy Grove later described the idea of Objectives and Key Results in the book *High Output Management* and posed two key questions, illustrated in Fig. 1.1: "Where do we want to go?" and "How do we know we have arrived?" At first glance, these two simple questions are the essence of Objectives and Key Results: Objectives and Key Results (Grove 1983).

John Doerr started at Intel in 1974, where he learned about Objectives and Key Results and found it helpful in his work, focusing on transparently communicated goals. As part of his later work as an investor for Kleiner Perkins, he introduced the model to Google founders Larry Page and Sergey Brin and the management team in 1999, where it is still an integral part today.

In 2013, Rick Klau, then a partner at Google Ventures, reported on how the Objectives and Key Results model is used at Google as part of a Startup Lab workshop, attracting attention outside Silicon Valley for the first time (Klau 2013).

Fig. 1.1 The essence of objectives and key results

Companies of all sizes and in all industries—including Amazon, Eventbrite, Gap, General Electric, GoPro, LinkedIn, Microsoft, Netflix, and X (formerly known as Twitter) in the United States; BMW, Deutsche Telekom, edeka, Flixbus, Metro, mymuesli, N26, Red Bull, SAP, Spotify, Telefonica, and Zalando in Europe; and Baidu, Blibli, Chumbak, Gojek, Midtrans, LG, Panasonic, and Samsung in Asia—use Objectives and Key Results to define their goals and measure their results.

The idea behind Objectives and Key Results is to help individuals or teams to focus on a small number of objectives and to define how to measure the achievement of these objectives within a manageable period of time. Objectives are qualitative and describe the "what" (what is to be achieved), and Key Results are quantitative and measure the "how" (how do we determine that the objectives have been achieved).

John Doerr has summarized this in a simple formula: We want to achieve <objective> and we measure that with <key result 1> and <key result 2> and <key result 3> (Grove 1983).

The objectives are described in a simple sentence. They define a specific target state that is to be achieved at the end of the period under review:

- Objectives are qualitative: Numbers have no place here because the objective defines the goal to be achieved at the end of the defined period. Vague terms such as "increase," "improve," "activate," "reduce," or "optimize" are not helpful here because, on the one hand, achievement cannot be measured and, on the other, even the smallest steps in the right direction could be mistaken for achieving the goal.
- Objectives are inspiring: Like the company's vision or mission statement, the objective should describe an ambitious (but achievable) future state. The focus is on the outcome, not the journey, and it should motivate people to get out of bed in the morning. Be bold—the OKRs are internal to the company and can be described in a language that is common to the team.
- Objectives are scheduled: Objectives are set for a manageable period of time—three months has proved to be a practical horizon and corresponds to thinking in quarters. Most projects are likely to be longer than a quarter, and it makes sense to break them down into milestones, as bulky topics are almost automatically broken down into chunks, making progress transparent.
- Objectives are derived: "Beyond" setting goals and measuring results for a relatively short period of time, say three months, there needs to be a clearly communicated direction for the organization. This answers the question of the organization's purpose. The organization's vision and mission, on the one hand, and its strategy, on the other, are the guiding lights against which objectives are set.
- Objectives are executable: For both fast-growing start-ups and established companies, it is important that the objectives of a team actually include the contribution of this team. The team must be able to achieve the contribution independently and without dependence on other parts of the organization within the agreed time frame. This ensures that the team can focus on its own goals while still keeping the company's goals in sight.

Well-formulated objectives include:

- Launch version 3.1 of the new product.
- Revolutionize the use of coupons on smartphones.

- Use of internal IT is perceived positively.
- Successful launch of the new monthly newsletter.
- Reduce the ordering process for cardboard boxes to five clicks.
- Develop an exceptional corporate culture.
- Set budget for the next financial year on time.
- Establish the best customer support in the industry.
- Develop our sales organization into the top team in the industry.
- Brand is perceived as the number one energy drink.

The Key Results quantify the previously defined objectives and make them measurable. They describe how the respective objectives are to be achieved:

- Key Results are ground-breaking: They are intended to answer the question "How do we know that we have achieved the agreed objectives?" and thus document the achievement in a way that is understandable and comprehensible for everyone. Well-formulated Key Results not only ensure that good results can be documented afterward, but also that new approaches and tools can be used to achieve objectives that were previously thought impossible.
- Key Results are measurable: Both the "before" expectations and the "after" results should be transparent, clearly defined, and communicated to all stakeholders at all times. Key Results are not the product of subjective opinions but allow clear decisions to be made as part of regular reviews as to what percentage they have been achieved.
- Key Results are achievable: The agreed targets should be ambitious but not impossible to achieve. We talk about a confidence level, which expresses confidence that the goal can be achieved within the agreed time frame—5 in 10 is a good start. 1 in 10 means it will take a miracle to get there, and 10 in 10 often means we are a little too sure it will be a walk in the park.
- Key Results are results-orientated: No matter how elaborate the activities and tasks, the achieved results should be described with the Key Results—the term itself gives an unmistakable hint. Terms such as "advise," "participate," or "analyze" describe activities and do not

necessarily help to agree on and validate an objectively measurable result with an appropriate metric.

- Key Results are independent: Each of the Key Results that are "linked" to the Objective and contribute to it should and can be achieved independently of the others. The usual dependences, milestones, or time sequences used in project planning do not lead to any meaningful Key Results. The achievement, non-achievement, or over-achievement of one Key Result must not affect the achievement and evaluation of the other Key Results.

Well-formulated Key Results include:

- Interviewed and presented 10 reference customers in ROI studies.
- Completed 70% of goods returned without human interaction.
- Finalized the beta version and showed it to 100 customers.
- 20 customers were surveyed monthly in a telephone interview.
- Free gym membership for all employees.
- The 10 most frequently asked questions are answered on the FAQ page.
- 5000 people subscribed to our blog.
- Two newsletters published per quarter.
- 1000 interested parties registered for the smartphone current account.
- Training program for new sales staff implemented.

Despite many controversial discussions about the details, different schools of thought have agreed on a useful value: About three Key Results should be defined for each Objective. For each Key Result, the outcome to be achieved and how the achievement of the Objective is to be measured are defined: This can be an absolute number, a change in a value, or a percentage.

The framework for working with OKR, for example, is a three-month cycle whose tasks are essentially the same from start to finish. In chronological order they are:

- Planning: This is where the objectives and corresponding Key Results for the entire cycle are defined—derived from the corporate vision and mission from "top-down" and the day-to-day business from "bottom-up."

- Weekly meetings: The current status of the Objectives and Key Results is discussed; the results and progress since the last meeting are made transparent.
- Review: At the end of the cycle, both objectives and achievements are evaluated against the metrics and expectations defined in the planning. It also provides a solid basis for planning the next cycle.
- Retrospective: This takes a systemic view of the OKR process and creates a space for team sharing and continuous improvement of the cycle, independent of the "hard facts" resulting from the review. Figure 1.2 shows this cycle at a glance.

The overall aim of the framework is to harmonize Objectives and expected Key Results in such a way that there is a common understanding of direction for the period of the three-month cycle, that all activities contribute to this direction, and that there is clarity about the resources required to achieve it.

Neither the approach nor the organizational framework can be successfully copied from the oft-cited pioneers Google, Twitter, and Zalando—an adaptation to the culture, history, and pace of your own organization is of course necessary. Roles, responsibilities, and ways of

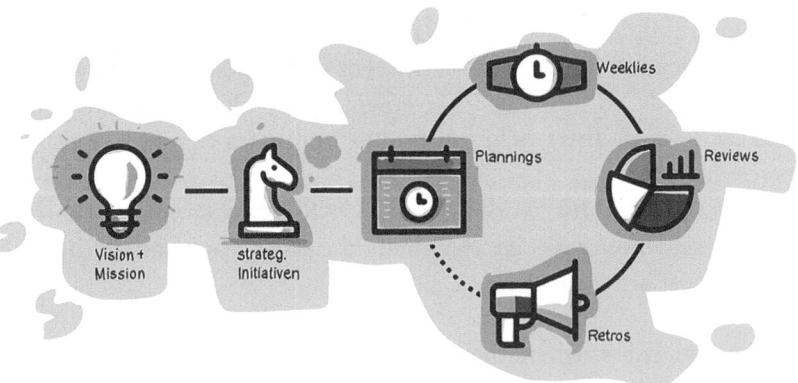

Fig. 1.2 OKR cycle

decision-making are always different in organizations of different sectors, sizes, and ages, and it is not always easy to rethink and adapt.

The OKR Master helps the organization to implement and apply the OKR and is the point of contact for questions about the method and the process. This person is the central point of contact in the company for planning and organization, supports those involved with methodological knowledge, and moderates planning, reviews, and retrospectives.

As a change agent, facilitator, coach, and subject matter expert, the OKR Master is the go-to person for both management and employees when it comes to implementing Objectives and Key Results across the organization. Ideally, the OKR Master is disciplinarily independent of the teams he or she supports and is not part of the organization's top management.

As the responsibility includes involving all stakeholders in the process, managing their expectations and concerns, and clarifying any misunderstandings, a talent for explaining what may initially be perceived as a complex process in an understandable way is required, along with high standards of good communication and genuine empathy.

The key principles of working with OKRs and the expected benefits can be described in three specific areas. These are the following:

- Focus and priorities: Once the goals and expected results have been defined, the focus of those involved is on achieving them. The manageable number of Objectives and the corresponding Key Results also ensures concentration on the essential topics. If OKRs are used for strategic projects and initiatives in the company—as is the case at Google—this ensures a focus on the most important issues. Topics that were not selected as part of the planning are not part of the activities of the current cycle.
- Transparency and clarity: Ideally, the OKRs of everyone involved in the company are publicly available. The priorities of teams and individuals are visible, and Objectives and Key Results that have little to do with the corporate vision and mission can be easily identified and possibly corrected. The "contribution" of one's own activities to the agreed goals and to the big picture becomes clear, and substantial

thoughts on one's own contribution have a positive effect on motivation.
- Decisions and coordination: Working with OKRs makes it unmistakably clear what is to be achieved in the current cycle. Projects and opportunities that suddenly arise and do not support the agreed goals can be rejected with better justification by referring to the Objectives and Results. The coordination of people and teams in the planning phase, combined with the allocation of resources to the topics, ensures that the available people and resources are used efficiently.

The primary goals are not necessarily rapid growth and process improvement at all costs. The framework and approach can act as a catalyst for real innovation, sustainable development of people and teams, and successful cultural change, especially in established organizations. OKRs link the organization's vision and mission to tangible Objectives and Key Results, creating clarity at all levels about strategy and direction and how the organization contributes to it.

1.3 OKRs and Their Neighborhood

What makes thinking in and working with Objectives and Key Results so special, what related or competing formats do we find, and what do they have in common? We describe five neighboring approaches that we believe are essential to understanding what we have in common and what separates us in the context of OKRs and that are important for formulating inspiring Objectives and comprehensible Key Results.

OKRs and Management Systems
Management systems that focus on the implementation of strategies and the achievement of objectives in organizations generally include the following steps:

- Define the organization's vision and mission.
- Define the strategy and business model.
- Translate the strategy into concrete plans.

- Execute plans and objectives in day-to-day operations.
- Plan and execute projects and initiatives.
- Define guidelines, frameworks, and standards.
- Measure and evaluate performance.

Objectives and Key Results focus on the operational steps in this list. They are an enormous help in translating the business strategy into concrete and understandable steps, and in executing and measuring the performance achieved. The breakdown of overall company objectives into team and individual objectives ensures greater transparency and a stronger focus on achieving short-term goals. The predefined and clearly quantifiable key results represent a significant development compared to traditional Management by Objectives—without agreeing on the corresponding results.

However, to map and manage the day-to-day business mentioned in the list above requires a good understanding of the current operational issues and an assessment of the actual effort involved, as well as a clear understanding that the high proportion of day-to-day business compared to projects and initiatives should be considered when agreeing and measuring Key Results.

The work of individuals and teams is assessed as part of the objectives and key results by evaluating the results at the end of the quarter. This makes it easy to give feedback on the previous quarter's work based on the percentage of objectives achieved, but this should never be linked to bonus schemes. The setting of achievable targets at the beginning of the quarter would suffer, as key results would be set much less ambitiously in order to hit the target line safely and receive a bonus for doing so or for exceeding the targets. As a result, the motivation to set realistic yet ambitious targets would be completely lost.

OKR and Management by Objectives
Although Andy Grove derived his idea of Objectives and Key Results from the Management by Objectives approach described in this chapter, there are three clear differences, particularly in terms of practical implementation, decades later:

- Management by Objectives focuses on defining what is to be achieved in the company. Results derived from this per Objective, similar to Key Results, are not included. This means that the What (what we want to achieve) is described, but not the How (how we will achieve the goal).
- The agreement of Management by Objectives between management and employees is usually confidential. The OKRs of teams and employees, on the other hand, are usually published within the organization and should be comprehensible to everyone involved at all times.
- Targets are agreed and monitored annually as part of Management by objectives. Targets are set "from top-down" and are usually linked to an employee performance appraisal and their variable salary components.

It is in the nature of the MBO that objectives are agreed with as little risk as possible, while the objectives and results agreed as part of the OKR cycle can and should be ambitious. If the How has been made transparent in the organization, the possibility of only partially achieving the agreed Key Results is "built in" and must not be sanctioned.

Management by Objectives is still practiced in many companies of different sizes and industries, but the clock is ticking: even Peter Drucker, the grandfather of Management by Objectives, is quoted as saying that MBOs are not the perfect cure for inefficient management.

OKR and Key Performance Indicators
The purpose of Key Performance Indicators is to measure and document the progress or achievement of an organization's most important objectives. It is rightly argued that they help to monitor the success of important activities within the organization.

However, as important as it is to measure indicators of effective processes and actions, it is equally important to select the really important indicators in order to maintain an overview—the term "key" in Key Performance Indicators is a clue! Key Performance Indicators and OKRs do not compete with each other, but complement each other perfectly:

- Key Performance Indicators measure results in clear numbers. For example, "number of attendees at monthly evening events" may be an important KPI for a coworking space provider when it comes to increasing the perception of the target group in a particular city.
- The Key Results describe how the respective goals are to be achieved and signal whether we have already arrived at our destination or are at least moving in the right direction on the way there. For example, the coworking space provider might have formulated the objective "The target group in Heidelberg perceives us as a relevant offer," and the corresponding Key Result might be "Increase the number of visitors by 20% from event to event."

This and many other real-life examples suggest that Key Performance Indicators are not in competition with Key Results, but are part of them: "Number of visitors" is clearly part of "Increase number of visitors by 20% from event to event."

Both have their place in well-functioning organizations. However, the focus should be on those metrics that actually contribute to the success of people, teams, and projects.

OKR and Lean Management

The idea and methods of Lean Management are not necessarily new. Its origins can be traced back to shipbuilding in Venice in the mid-fifteenth century, and Henry Ford adapted the idea of lean production in Michigan around 1910. The Japanese Kiichiro Toyoda and Taiichi Ohno revolutionized production in the 1950s with the Toyota Production System.

Although the core of the concept comes from the manufacture of physical products, Lean Management has helped many organizations of different sizes and industries to become leaner and faster. Service providers, non-profit organizations, and public authorities have all benefited from the approach, as have start-ups using the concept of lean start-up and agile development with short development cycles and rapid learning from customer requirements and market needs.

Indeed, the Lean Management approach can help to define Objectives and Key Results. At first glance, however, the difference is obvious: what characterizes Lean Management is a clear focus on efficiency. Properly thought through and applied, it ensures that the company's operations and processes flow in an optimal, continuous stream, eliminating unnecessary interfaces and eliminating waste.

Big leaps with ambitious goals, which we want to plan and achieve with the help of Objectives and Key Results, are not planned. However, Lean Management can certainly help to formulate good Objectives. The lean principles described by James Womack and Daniel Jones in 1996 can be easily "translated" to work with objectives and key results (Womack and Jones 2000):

- Lean principle 1: Let's define value from the perspective of our customers at the end of the value chain. This means that internal or external customers decide how concrete value is created and how lean and efficient a process is. They judge whether we deliver the right product or service at the right time and to the right quality.
- Lean principle 2: Let's identify the value stream. If we really want to improve processes, we need to consider all activities and stakeholders from start to finish. Again, our customers ultimately judge where value is created. All parts of the organization are put to the test to see where resources are wasted.
- Lean principle 3: Let's ensure continuous flow. By consciously eliminating non-value-adding activities and waste, a flow is created without major interruptions and waiting times. The aim is to organize the individual steps of the process in a meaningful sequence and to reduce interfaces.
- Lean principle 4: Give our customers what they need, when they need it. Instead of "pushing" process steps through the organization regardless of demand and available capacity, the entire process is "pulled" upstream by the customer. The result is that we produce only what our customers want.
- Lean principle 5: Let's strive for perfection. This is undoubtedly the essence and North Star of Lean Management, whether in production, project management, or administration. This quest for perfection—whether we call it Kaizen or the continuous improvement process—is systematic, incremental, and probably never finished.

Let's try to "translate" the five lean principles into five OKR principles in a nutshell. They provide a perfect basis for defining motivating Objectives and comprehensible Key Results:

- OKR principle 1: Let's define Objectives as the answer to what creates real value for our customers and our organization. Objectives must be linked to our organization's mission in a way that is understandable to all stakeholders at all times.
- OKR principle 2: We will review and revise any formulation for Key Results statements that do not provide value to customers. Let's create clear "evidence" that the agreed objectives have been achieved. This evidence must be available and verifiable to all stakeholders at all times.
- OKR principle 3: Let's ensure that the defined Objectives are translated into a series of measurable milestones. These milestones must clearly contribute to the agreed objectives. Let's review milestones that contribute little or nothing to the objectives.
- OKR principle 4: Let's design communication according to the pull principle and "pull" the Objectives and related Key Results through the organization. Agreements start at the corporate level and continue through the team level to the individual employee.
- OKR principle 5: Let's strive for focus. The implementation of Objectives and Key Results is unlikely to be perfect in the first cycle; it usually takes two or three rounds before the planning effort is significantly reduced. The aim is to focus on the really important issues.

Translating the company's vision and mission into inspiring goals and measurable results leads to a reduction in activities that contribute little to the company's direction and in Lean Management is referred to as wasted resources. Even though perfection will probably never be achieved, the first positive effects of focusing on the important activities can be seen quickly as soon as we start the journey.

OKR and Start with Why

Working with Objectives and Key Results has undoubtedly proven to be an effective way to focus many organizations of different revenue models, sizes, maturity levels, and industries—in some cases for decades. The contribution of teams and individuals to the achievement of organizational goals becomes clearer, decisions are easier to make, and the cascade of goals from top to bottom and back becomes more transparent.

However, agreeing objectives and tracking key results does not necessarily ensure that the "right" objectives are set. Goals do not answer the question of Why or to What end an organization should pursue them. The question of what makes individuals, teams, or organizations do what they do is not necessarily answered by objectives.

Most of the examples of Objectives and Key Results mentioned in Sect. 1.2 were formulated by established companies. These companies have usually known for a long time Why they do what they do, even if it is not always expressed explicitly and succinctly. However, recent conversations and coaching sessions the authors have had with clients show that few founders and leaders of small and medium-sized enterprises are able to articulate their Why in a way that is understandable and invites participation or investment. One could argue that this Why—the drive—is hidden in the company's mission. The authors find that it is often all too well hidden and in many organizations is either poorly communicated, long forgotten, or incomprehensibly formulated.

In his 2009 bestseller, *Start with Why*, Simon Sinek describes the Golden Circle shown in Fig. 1.3, with Why at its center (Sinek 2009). The How in the second layer describes the processes of an organization, and the What in the third layer describes the products or services an organization provides.

At first glance, he suggests a very simple formula to help formulate the Why: **<contribution>, in order to < effect>**. His own Why is formulated as follows: "We want to inspire people to do what inspires them, so that together we can change the world." His contribution is inspiration, and the impact is changing the world together.

According to Simon Sinek—and confirmed by the authors' experience in many workshops—the Why leads to a better understanding of what inspires and motivates us: Why does a company exist? Why do we get up in the morning? Why should someone be interested in what we have to offer?

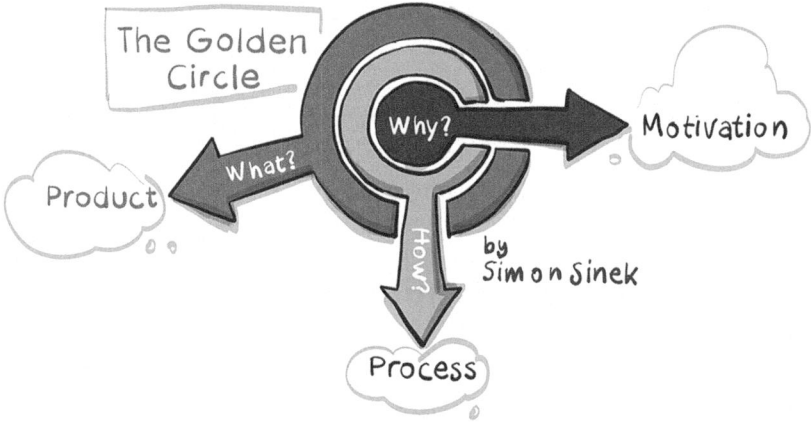

Fig. 1.3 Golden Circle

This Why is both the starting point and the North Star when it comes to formulating inspiring goals and transparent results. The organization's Objectives and Key Results can be derived from the Golden Circle, often more concretely and tangibly than from the company's mission and vision. There are currently several interpretations of a meaningful link between the Golden Circle and the Objectives and Key Results, some of which contradict each other. The authors propose this link:

- The Why sets the direction: It has not yet been determined whether and which products or services will support the Why, or which processes will be necessary and useful to produce and deliver them. The Why is the identity and provides the drive and motivation. It is the starting point for deriving the objectives and key results.
- The How is the bridge between the Why and the What: it describes an organization's business model and processes. This is where the company's unique selling proposition lies and where the agreed values and principles can be found. The Objectives and Key Results defined at company level and the How must be consistent.
- The What describes the company's offering: the products or services and therefore the concrete results of the Why and How. The What is the part of the Golden Circle that is visible and tangible outside the

company and, according to the authors, does not provide a meaningful link to the Objectives and Key Results.

Being inspired by a clear Why, deriving Objectives and Key Results from this—and carefully synchronizing these with the How—will lead to goals that are actually worth starting with.

1.4 Cases and Applications

With the following four examples, the authors want to make working with objectives and key results more tangible and invite you to apply them to your organization. The companies, their backgrounds, and the use of Objectives and Key Results are real and anonymized. In order to provide useful examples and keep the focus on the essentials, we have focused on three Objectives and three Key Results for each of the companies considered.

- Example 1—HEDAKU: The company will produce treats for pets. With a clear link to a city with a positive image and 12 million tourists a year, and a niche to fill, it will offer a product that dogs and their owners don't need but want.
- Example 2—BRNHLD: The company advises founders, not-for-profit organizations, and mid-sized companies on the steps from the idea to a robust, well-tested business model and helps them find a serious answer to the exciting question of why customers buy.
- Example 3—AVATAR: The company's product creates a unique symbiosis of art and technology for relaxation and stress reduction. The sculpture, which is produced in small series, helps people to activate their own resources by providing biofeedback through the visualization of heart rate.
- Example 4—VISUAL: For almost 15 years, the company has been providing graphic recordings of conferences, workshops, and keynote speeches for medium-sized businesses, non-profit organizations, and corporations in German-speaking countries, as well as illustrations for books, white papers, and presentations.

As explained in Sect. 1.1, Objectives are described in a single sentence and define a specific target state to be achieved at the end of the period. They are expressed in qualitative terms and are ideally both achievable and inspiring.

Key Results quantify the previously defined Objectives and make them measurable. They describe how the objectives are to be achieved within the defined timeframe and should be feasible and consistently result-oriented.

The Objectives and Key Results of HEDAKU

The founders have set themselves objectives for the first quarter that are closely linked to the development of the brand, the production of the first product and packaging prototypes, and the simultaneous launch of communications. These are as follows:

- Objective 1: A solid organizational framework is in place.
  - Key Result 1: The five most relevant social media channels and the three most relevant channels for German-language podcasts are "reserved" with usernames.
  - Key Result 2: The domain is connected to one.com and will be redirected to an existing website until the sales launch.
  - Key Result 3: The word mark application has been received by the German Patent and Trade Mark Office and can be found in the online register.

- Objective 2: An exciting brand is prepared.
  - Key Result 1: The product stories for ten similar offers are compiled.
  - Key Result 2: The product story is written in a testable version of about 100 words.
  - Key Result 3: The logo is designed in a near-series quality to be tested among friends.

- Objective 3: A "likeable" product is designed.
  - Key Result 1: All authorities relevant for production approval are identified, including direct contact persons.

- Key Result 2: Five different prototypes of the product are ready to be tested in a close environment.
- Key Result 3: A decision is made whether to manufacture in-house or outsource, and a short list of three possible manufacturers is drawn up.

The Objectives and Key Results of BRNHLD

The consultant has defined Objectives for the second quarter that focus on the development and integration of a promising new offering into the existing ones, plus proactive communication of the company's brand. These are as follows:

- Objective 1: More fun—we have a lot of joy with our offerings.
  - Key Result 1: Our Why is formulated clearly and comprehensibly.
  - Key Result 2: Two episodes of our new podcast are live.
  - Key Result 3: A contract with a top 10 publisher is signed.
- Objective 2: Increase revenue—all products generate good revenue.
  - Key Result 1: Q4 revenue is higher than Q4 in 2023.
  - Key Result 2: Pipeline for Q4 + Q1 is higher than the revenue in 2023.
  - Key Result 3: Three new partner companies have been acquired.
- Objective 3: Greater reach—we are being noticed.
  - Key Result 1: Presentations on two important offerings are being tested.
  - Key Result 2: A catchy name for our new offering has been found.
  - Key Result 3: We have 250 references on a reputable review portal.

The Objectives and Key Results of AVATAR

The owner's objectives for the first quarter are the successful start of low volume production after a long prototype phase and the next necessary steps. These are as follows:

- Objective 1: An alternative supplier is found.
  - Key Result 1: A short list of three potential suppliers is completed.

- Key Result 2: A detailed design for version 2.0 is available.
- Key Result 3: A reliable cost estimate has been obtained.

• Objective 2: My marketing strategy is designed.

- Key Result 1: A contract with a strategic partner has been signed.
- Key Result 2: A first announcement mentioning the collaboration is live.
- Key Result 3: An authentic and engaging story about the product is online.

• Objective 3: I have fun with my customers.

- Key Result 1: I made visits to 20 new customers.
- Key Result 2: I received ten new testimonials with names and roles.
- Key Result 3: I have gained five new customers through referrals.

The Objectives and Key Results of VISUAL

The Managing Director has set targets for the fourth quarter of the current year that focus on the structured search for promising technologies while expanding the existing range. These are as follows:

• Objective 1: I discover new business areas.

- Key Result 1: Two "fine arts" live illustrations are sold.
- Key Result 2: My "fun products" have earned me 1000 euros.
- Key Result 3: The plan to focus on storytelling is completed.

• Objective 2: My publications earn money.

- Key Result 1: My draft for a comic book is finished.
- Key Result 2: The contract for a workbook is signed.
- Key Result 3: The third edition of my first book is available.

• Objective 3: I will take the next technological steps.

- Key Result 1: The drawing robot has been used live twice.
- Key Result 2: AR hardware and applications are being tested.
- Key Result 3: I evaluated three new drawing apps.

1.5 Key Takeaways

Implementing Objectives and Key Results is an effort that can be hard to justify for your organization—whether you are part of a start-up, a medium-sized company, or a large corporation. However, the authors believe that this investment in time and money is well worth it. Why is this and what are the concrete benefits?

The benefits for employees:

- One's own contribution becomes visible when the individual's goals and the organization's goals are largely aligned. When issues change in the organization, the change in priorities becomes transparent.
- The big picture becomes clearer when the organization's goals are transparent at all times. Management decisions are easier to understand, and employees are more involved in the process of setting goals.
- Saying "no" to additional topics becomes easier because the current tasks are derived from the current quarter's OKR list. For each new task, a different one should be taken from the list.

The benefits for managers:

- The focus is on the topics agreed at the beginning of the quarter in the form of Objectives and Key Results. Issues that are not part of the OKR are not planned until the next round.
- The results and achievements are measurable because the Key Results are derived from the Objectives. Both are defined at the beginning of the quarter and measured at the end of the period in terms of target achievement.
- Communication becomes more transparent as everyone involved is aware of their own Objectives and those of other people and teams at all times. The definition of Objectives and Key Results also takes place through intensive dialogue.

The benefits for founders and owners:

- The corporate vision is consistently translated into inspiring short-term goals and measurable results. This ensures that the entire organization is working in a common direction.
- Decisions about scarce resources in the business become easier as they are deployed in a planned way. These resources are allocated as part of the goal-setting process at the beginning of a quarter.
- There is less risk of chasing resource-draining distractions because they cannot override the activities planned for the period. This means that the really important issues can be moved forward.

References

Doerr, John. 2018. *Measure what matters*. New York: Penguin Random House.
Doran, George. 1981. There's a S.M.A.R.T. way to write management's goals and objectives. In *Management review*, ed. Anthony Rutigliano, 35–26. New York: American Management Association.
Grove, Andrew. 1983. *High output management*. New York: Penguin Random House.
Klau, Rick. 2013. How Google sets goals: OKRs. www.youtube.com/watch?v=mJB83EZtAjc. Accessed 1 June 2024.
Locke, Edwin. 1968. Toward a theory of task motivation and incentives. www.sciencedirect.com/science/article/abs/pii/0030507368900044?via%3Dihub. Accessed 1 June 2024.
Sinek, Simon. 2009. *Start with why—How great leaders inspire everyone to take action*. New York: Portfolio Penguin.
Womack, James, and Jones, Daniel. 2000. Principles of Lean. www.lean.org/lexicon-terms/lean-thinking-and-practice. Accessed 1 June 2024.

2

Why LEGO SERIOUS PLAY?

In this section, the authors invite you to find out more about the origins and scientific background of LEGO SERIOUS PLAY. You will also learn about the activating format and become familiar with the application through real-life examples.

2.1 Background and Building Blocks

"Tomorrow, I will continue where we left off today: I will reach out (points to the hands of two LEGO minifigures) to those who have not yet understood the change. But I am also ready to fight the destructive ones (touches the sword of a minifigure representing an otherwise peaceful king). I'm sure we can do it because you're behind me (points to a line of minifigures set up behind the king)."

This was the client's summary of a workshop: the company asked itself and the authors the exciting question of how to define Objectives in a comprehensible way and agree on Key Results. We found relevant answers with the help of an analogue application that makes it possible to think together, build together, and find digital future scenarios for companies. Figure 2.1 shows the client inserting his model into a landscape.

Why start by organizing key people into small groups, ignoring any evidence of their perceived lack of creativity, and guiding them through a tight agenda over several days? Because together we want to bring to the table the issues that matter in times of rapid change. Because we want real results. Because we want to create orientation. Because we want to derive practical decision-making aids for a future that is uncertain but can be shaped.

We call this Strategic Preparedness, and by this we mean nothing less than "being prepared as an organization"—including being prepared for

- Future events that we cannot yet know
- Further disruptions, the effects of which we cannot foresee
- Emerging competitors that we have not yet identified

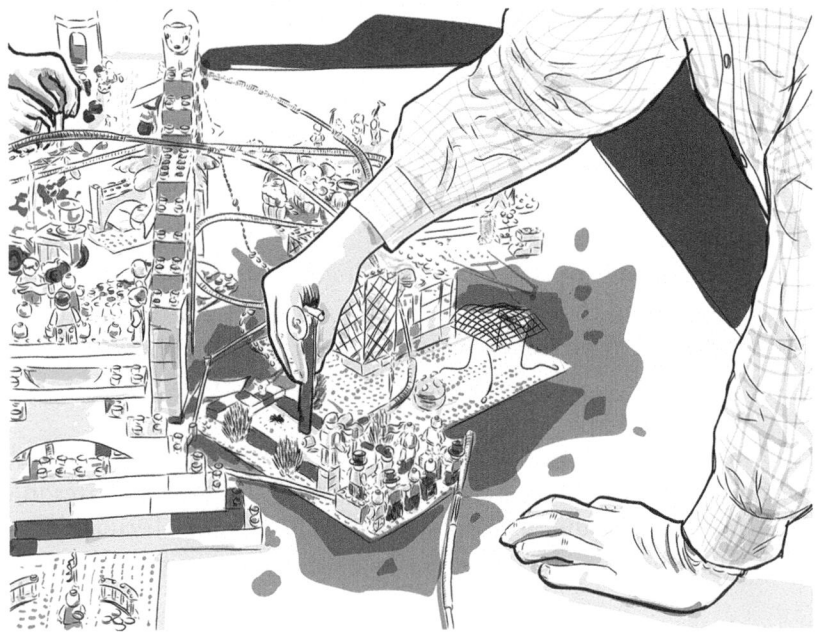

Fig. 2.1 Creating and discussing a common image

- Unknown products that will transform entire industries

The knowledge and experience of individuals becomes the knowledge and experience of the whole organization. Knowledge, experience, and new insights are shared, and this ensures that the organization develops a stable and resilient confidence that it can achieve its objectives and deliver truly useful results, even in uncertain times.

Greater insight into the current situation of entire industries and greater confidence in being able to contribute to a positive future—or several possible "futures"—with understandable goals do not in itself add value. Only when all participants agree to translate the findings and results into concrete steps and actually take them will the underlying question of the workshop be answered: The aim must be for everyone to agree on these next steps.

The common work is done when:

- New insights into the current situation of the organization are gained.
- The knowledge of all those involved is shared in such a way that it becomes tangible.
- The team is confident that it can act on this knowledge.
- All parties involved agree in principle to this action.
- The organization is prepared to respond to future issues.

The central aim of the concept is to support organizations of different sizes and structures to understand complex structures and processes more clearly than before, in order to be better prepared for future challenges. This requires the efforts of key personnel who do not want to hear the same empty phrases over and over again, but who want to discuss realizable strategies and communicate them credibly to employees, partners, and customers.

The concept is implemented through an intensive workshop of at least one day, during which a picture is created of the organization and, for example, customers, prospects, partners, suppliers, competitors, and investors. Workshop participants use this to test scenarios and possible futures: Roles, relationships, and processes are discussed using three-dimensional LEGO models, changing over the course of the workshop and providing a solid basis for future decisions.

These components form the basis for surprising insights and tangible results when it comes to navigating in an uncertain environment:

- Storytelling and the use of metaphors
- Mihaly Csíkszentmihályi's flow and Kurt Hahn's idea of creative passion (schöpferische Leidenschaft)
- Imagination

Storytelling and working with metaphors are the keys to shaping the future of a business. When children play and tell stories, ordinary objects and materials are transformed into people, animals, vehicles, and all sorts of other creatures. Not just for children: Myths, legends, and fairy tales have always been used by adults to express ideals and values. In (re)telling stories, we deal with issues such as culture, religion, social and personal identity, or belonging to a group. Through storytelling we are easily able to make sense of and understand our social, cultural, and interpersonal "material." Figure 2.2 shows a participant explaining her LEGO model.

Applied to the derivation of goals and corresponding results from the company's vision and mission, this means that stories contribute to the production, reproduction, and transformation—including the deconstruction—of new business models. Narratives fulfill a number of tasks: socializing new employees, legitimizing loyalty, and identification with the company. They act as a magnifying glass through which the organization's activities can be viewed, understood, and interpreted. Stories and metaphors are our vehicles for creating radically new ways of understanding.

Flow—the feeling of being completely absorbed in an activity, a rush of creativity and activity—arises in the area between overload or anxiety and underload or boredom. In a state of flow, there is complete harmony between the aforementioned limbic system, which controls emotions, and the cortical system, which controls consciousness and reason.

What happens in the process?

Fig. 2.2 Building models and telling stories

- We are able to concentrate on what we do.
- There is a good balance between requirements and skills.
- Neither boredom nor excessive demands arise.
- We are in control of our activity.
- Action and awareness merge.

In practical terms, Mihaly Csíkszentmihályi's theory of flow means that what we create ends up in our heads and stays there, so that jointly found images of new ideas, concepts, and products can be passed on effortlessly and credibly (Csíkszentmihályi 2010).

The experiential educator Kurt Hahn, who founded Schloss Salem—the most famous boarding school in the German-speaking world—together with Prince Max von Baden, called this flow experience "creative passion" more than a hundred years ago. The third of the Seven Salem Laws he formulated was and still is: "Give the children the opportunity of self-effacement in the common cause" (Hahn 1930).

Herein lies the key to navigating an uncertain environment:

- Self-effacement: Confidence in one's own abilities almost inevitably leads to greater initiative, motivation, and commitment to the goal.
- Common cause: The creation of a common image on which all participants agree after a stimulating and, admittedly, exhausting dialogue.

Figure 2.3 shows how the concept of "creating a common picture" is brought to life: Participants work together to build a landscape that represents the current situation of a corporate department.

Imagination can be interpreted in different ways: "visualizing" or "imagining" something. In the context of preparing for digital transformation, imagination can have three meanings:

- Describing something
- Creating something
- Questioning something

Fig. 2.3 Flow happens when creating and discussing a common picture

The interplay of these three forms is what Strategic Imagination is all about—the origin of creative, radical, unusual new ideas for viable responses to change.

Descriptive Imagination creates images that describe a complex and often confusing environment. It recognizes clear patterns and regularities in a flood of information—roughly the more realistic form of *The Matrix* movie. Examples include value chains, Kim and Mauborgne's four-action format, or the Boston Consulting Group's BCG matrix (Kim and Mauborgne 2005). With Descriptive Imagination we see what is happening before our eyes and put it into context. It is particularly useful for creating a shared understanding of the current situation as a starting point for new strategies.

Creative Imagination is needed to develop strategies and business models—brainstorming and many large group facilitation methods are examples of this. While Descriptive Imagination helps us to recognize what the current state of affairs is, Creative Imagination allows us to see what is not there—and thus to create something truly new and different. The result is innovative strategies where companies try to sideline their competitors rather than compete directly with them—Google, Dell, Slack, Airbnb, and Uber are great examples of this.

Challenging Imagination radically contradicts and even destroys the usual idea of progress and speed for speed's sake. It throws out all the outdated rules and clears the air. It does not simply add a small new element to an existing one; it starts from scratch and assumes nothing. The term "deconstruction" best describes this phenomenon. A good example of this is Michael Hammer's approach to reengineering: it is not about improving existing practices, but about "abandonment and new beginnings, starting with the proverbial clean slate and redefining one's work and approach," as Hammer puts it (Hammer and Stanton 1995).

All three together make up Strategic Imagination—a process made up of these previously discussed forms of imagination. As a desirable side effect, it creates a social dynamic: new knowledge is constructed with previously learned knowledge and experience. New meanings emerge from this knowledge, and a clear direction is created with shared answers.

This approach is radically different from conventional approaches to idea generation, idea consolidation, and idea selection, where often not all participants have the opportunity to contribute their own insights, skills, and experiences that are important for a common picture. Playful approaches such as LEGO SERIOUS PLAY create a level playing field for all participants from the very first minute and ensure more attention, more fun, more participation, and better results when it comes to real innovation in organizations.

"I don't always have to have the last word (laughter in the workshop room). The important thing is that we now have a unified approach (points to the polar bear labelled 'Balance' at the top of a sturdy LEGO bridge) that has been jointly formulated and that everyone is behind. We will change as part of the digital wave (picks up the DUPLO whale from the landscape and holds it up to the camera) and we will take the employees with us. It is also important that we have recognized that we are in this together—and that we have no doubt that we will succeed."

This is the summary of the workshop mentioned above: with the guidelines developed for cooperation between managers and the derivation of Objectives and Key Results, the organization has built a solid foundation that prepares it well for the future.

What helps to finally make use of the knowledge available in companies, to make processes and structures radically tangible, and thus to prepare the organization for navigating "by sight"?

- Tools and procedures that recognize that an organization's environment changes faster than traditional planning and strategy development processes
- Tools and procedures that ensure that an organization is optimally prepared for change with unpredictable outcomes
- Tools and procedures that therefore need to provide a set of guidelines that are co-designed, supported, and understood by all those involved

This is the only way to achieve meaningful results in the long term. These guidelines provide a framework for improving the quality of key decisions in the pursuit of understandable and achievable goals. They ensure that the agreed direction is followed by enabling key people in the organization to develop a set of functional tools to respond quickly and

2 Why LEGO SERIOUS PLAY?

Fig. 2.4 Steering the ship and its occupants past the danger

effectively to deviations. Figure 2.4 shows how workshop participants responded to the question about guard rails for the organization in the face of expected events.

2.2 Your First Steps in 3D

Research and countless workshops with real questions and actionable results have clearly shown that the behavior of people involved in innovation processes changes significantly and irreversibly positively when the triad of thinking, feeling, and moving is "built in." The results show that insights and experiences remain "hard-wired" in the memory for a long time because the limbic system, which is particularly important for processing experiences, is stimulated. The interface between the different brain systems recognizes which information is new, coordinates the content, and organizes the storage of this now conscious information from working memory into long-term memory.

Building on the LEGO SERIOUS PLAY concept, which has been continuously developed since the late 1990s, the authors make use of several "intelligences" of the workshop participants: the approach stimulates their visual, auditory, and kinesthetic abilities. The participants discover directly that they already knew what they did not know. Through the tight choreography of the workshop and the use of this haptic method, buried and intrinsic knowledge becomes tangible and can be recalled in the future.

The consistent sequence of:

- Build models in response to the questions formulated by the facilitator
- Give meaning to the models
- Tell the "story" about the model you have built

supports this by repeatedly sharing each person's individual knowledge and experience. All participants have the opportunity to share their own views without being influenced beforehand by faster and louder group members. This is the only way to create a shared picture that allows effective work on viable strategies, promising business models and possible futures.

This approach is based on a few important key assumptions:

- Even managers in an organization do not have all the answers; the implementation of agreed goals depends on listening to all voices in the room.
- People in an organization want to be part of a larger whole and take responsibility for good and bad results.
- All those involved can and should contribute to the future development of their organization by having their say, listening, and participating.
- The success and sustainability of a solution depends on everyone in the room being heard.
- Knowledge and experience are not always optimally distributed in organizations, which has an impact on the results derived from the objectives.

These assumptions have been translated into the consistent sequence described above, which the developers of the method call the core process. The core process consists of four steps:

- Step 1—Posing the question: The facilitator asks the workshop participants an open-ended question, called a challenge, to which there is no single correct or obvious answer. The question must be clear and understandable so that there are no misunderstandings about its interpretation.
- Step 2—Building a model: Each participant builds a LEGO model in response to the previously posed question. There are no restrictions on the number, type, or color of LEGO bricks used. However, the facilitator usually sets a time limit for building.
- Step 3—Sharing the story: Each participant presents the model they have built and the story behind it. It is important that all participants really tell the story of their model and receive full attention.
- Step 4—Reflecting on the story: Workshop participants reflect on their own and others' stories. The combination of the models and the explanations creates three-dimensional metaphors that are well anchored in the minds of all participants for a long time.

The "built-in" benefits of this core process are that all workshop participants, without exception, are involved in formulating their own thoughts and shared insights and in finding solutions, the risk of misunderstandings and misinterpretations is minimized, and the focus is placed more on the statements and less on the person.

First Warm-Up Exercise
When workshop participants are using the LEGO SERIOUS PLAY method and materials for the first time, reactions can range from "That sounds like fun, let's get started!" to "How can playing with LEGO bricks help me work on my goals?" A gentle introduction to working with the sometimes-unfamiliar special collection of LEGO bricks and the agenda is particularly important in order to create willingness to work with this method and trust in the approach and the facilitator.

The above sequence of three steps consisting of:

- Building models in response to a question
- Giving meaning to these models
- Telling the "story" about the model that has been built

is run through in a kind of warm-up program in order to meet the different expectations of the clients—regarding the relevance of the method, the process, or the topic of OKR in general—and experiences—with creative approaches in general, with previously tried methods or with other facilitators and consultants—and to provide sufficient security for the subsequent work together.

The LEGO SERIOUS PLAY Starter Kit with order number 2000414 and around 230 bricks, available online from the LEGO website under the SERIOUS PLAY theme, is perfect for getting started and then working on objectives. After the warm-up phase of the workshop, it is advisable to add the Identity and Landscape Kit. This can be found under order number 2000430 and contains approximately 2800 bricks. Combining the two sets will stimulate the participants' creativity. Figure 2.5 shows the contents of the LEGO SERIOUS PLAY Starter Kit.

The idea behind the first exercise is to get to know both the tool—the special set of LEGO bricks—and the process—the sequence of building models, giving meaning, telling a story. The facilitator creates a safe environment in which the workshop participants feel comfortable to enter into an open dialogue and trust each other and the facilitator.

The authors revisit the core process and use it to describe the steps of the first exercise:

- Step 1—Posing the question: The challenge formulated by the facilitator is to use some of the bricks to build a tower as tall as you can. Framing the task in terms of which bricks are to be used, which brick is to form the base of the tower, and what is to form the top of the tower helps to get into the flow state mentioned in Sect. 3.1 more quickly and to create an initial sense of success with a question that is perceived as harmless.

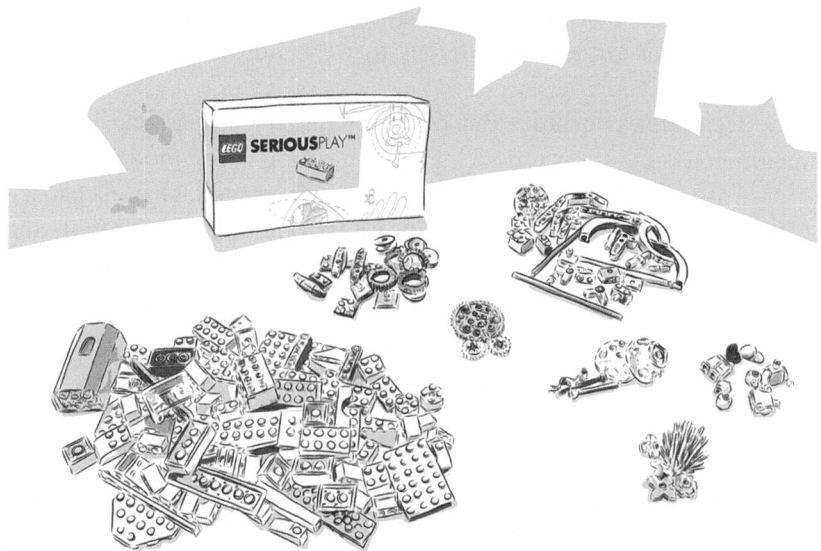

Fig. 2.5 LSP Starter Kit

- Step 2—Building a model: The workshop participants each build a tower out of LEGO bricks as an answer. There are no restrictions on the LEGO bricks to be used, other than the framework previously formulated by the facilitator. A time frame of about 3–4 min has proved to be feasible in order to build a tower in a relaxed yet focused manner.
- Step 3—Telling the story: The workshop participants present the tower to each other, spending no more than 1 min each. All participants, without exception, tell the story of their model. Everyone else listens carefully to the presenter to understand the meaning of the model. The facilitator either asks who wants to start presenting the tower or suggests a sequence. This step is central because it is not so much the elegance of the model but the meaning of the model that is essential to the process.
- Step 4—Reflecting on the story: In addition to their own story about their tower, workshop participants also reflect on the stories of others. The questions about the model formulated by the facilitator or the other participants after each presentation help here. The towers, which

are likely to be very different, clearly show that the same question and the same tools can lead to different answers and that this is OK.

The facilitator concludes the first exercise by emphasizing how the same process—building a model, giving meaning to the model, telling a story—ensures that a kind of new language is created, that all participants have a say, and that a common understanding of a situation and possible future developments is created. Figure 2.6 shows a workshop participant explaining her tower.

Second Warm-Up Exercise
The second exercise introduces metaphors. The purpose of metaphors is not only to make communication clearer and easier to understand, but also richer, deeper, and more emotionally appealing. They are an essential tool for conveying ideas in a vivid and comprehensible way and for increasing linguistic expressiveness.

Fig. 2.6 Giving meaning to your LEGO creation

In order to ensure that all workshop participants have the same starting conditions, the facilitator should have the following picture of an airplane created, as shown in Figs. 2.7, 2.8, 2.9, and 2.10.

Only when all workshop participants have built the model does the facilitator ask everyone to change the model as a disruption and then transform it into a metaphor.

The authors return to the core process and use it to describe the steps of the first exercise:

- Step 1—Posing the question: The facilitator asks the participants to remove the last brick they added to the airplane. When they have done this, he asks them to turn the airplane on its back and add a black brick (any brick). The workshop participants should now change the model so that it shows, as a metaphor, how the adapted model will represent their organization or team (depending on the workshop context) in 5 years' time.

Fig. 2.7 The LEGO plane—step 1

Fig. 2.8 The LEGO plane—step 2

Fig. 2.9 The LEGO plane—step 3

Fig. 2.10 The LEGO plane—step 4

- Step 2—Building a model: Workshop participants are not restricted in their choice of bricks. The time frame is a maximum of 2 min. The short time frame is important so that workshop participants focus on the metaphor and not so much on how to realize the metaphor.
- Step 3—Sharing the story: Workshop participants explain their models. In general, the metaphors make the stories more relaxed and humorous. The facilitator makes sure that everyone listens to the builders. The facilitator may ask questions about some of the models so that the workshop participants can refer back to the questions later.
- Step 4—Reflecting on the story: In addition to their own stories, workshop participants also reflect on the stories of others. This challenge is not about the strategic direction of the team or organization, but about how metaphors help us to communicate and how clear the stories of colleagues become with metaphor and model.

Third Warm-Up Exercise

The aim of the third exercise, once we have become familiar with the process and the tools, is to become more familiar with what LEGO SERIOUS PLAY facilitators call "story making." When we tell stories, we take others on a journey. We convey complex information in and between the lines in an exciting way. The issues that are important to an organization's present and possible future become tangible and easy to communicate and share. The authors revisit the core process and use it to describe the steps in the third exercise:

- Step 1—Posing the question: The challenge formulated by the facilitator is to build a picture of an ideal customer from the bricks. Alternatives would be images of ideal colleagues, ideal business partners, or ideal lecturers. The facilitator instructs the participants to focus on the characteristics of the people. These should always be ideal concepts of a person and not real people. In the second exercise, building and sharing is also more important than a result that perfectly reflects reality. The focus is on letting your imagination run wild and creating a kind of three-dimensional metaphor as an answer to the question.
- Step 2—Building a model: The participants build their model from LEGO bricks. There are no restrictions on the number or type of LEGO bricks for the third exercise. A time frame of 5–6 min is perfect for building your own vision of an ideal customer in a relaxed yet focused way.
- Step 3—Sharing the story: The participants present their models to each other again, spending about 3 min on each one. Without exception, all participants tell the story of their model and everyone else listens attentively. Compared to the first exercise, the stories become more personal and concrete because it is the participants' own idea of an ideal customer that is explained. The facilitator creates space for other participants to ask questions about the model. This ensures that participants find and share further details worth mentioning in their own models.
- Step 4—Reflecting on the story: Workshop participants again reflect on their own story about their ideal of a person or organization and

the stories of others. Once again, the very different ideals of customers, colleagues, partners, or lecturers show that the same question and the same tools can lead to different answers and that this is okay. The same sequence of activities always makes it easier to bring one's own point of view to the table, even on fuzzy, difficult, or even uncomfortable issues.

The facilitator concludes the third exercise by emphasizing how the sequence practiced in the successive exercises will ensure that one's own views are clearly expressed, that previously unspoken views are shared, and that one's own and others' thoughts are built upon. Figure 2.11 shows the model of an ideal customer built with bricks from the LEGO SERIOUS PLAY Starter Kit.

Fig. 2.11 The ideal customer from the perspective of an internal consultant

2.3 Cases and Applications

A good example of the sustainable benefits of working with elements of LEGO SERIOUS PLAY is creating a shared view of an organization's most important customers. Whenever there are many voices in the room, each contributing their own perspective—that of product development, sales, research, marketing, controlling, management—with the best of intentions, it is worth working in three dimensions.

The Customer Jobs Canvas, developed and extensively tested by two of the authors, has become a useful two-dimensional format for many industries (Ematinger and Schulze 2018). It helps founders and departments of established companies to "think from the customer's perspective" in a structured and fast way, and to consider ideas for products and services less in terms of their technical advantages or components and more from the perspective of the potential customer.

Among other things, the canvas provides an overview of

- The functional, emotional, and social jobs to be performed by prospects and customers
- The spatial, temporal, or organizational context in which these persons find themselves
- Competing products and services that prospects and customers are currently using or have used
- The forces and phenomena that attract customers to a new offer or deter them from a new offer
- The clear disadvantages of its own offering and the benchmark for a good result from the customer's perspective

and, thus, makes it easier to understand what motivates the most important customers to buy a product or service. Figure 2.12 shows the structure of the canvas.

The number of building blocks in the canvas and the underlying questions to be answered can seem daunting without the support of experienced facilitators. The somewhat vague concept of the customer's "task," referred to as the "job-to-be-done," does not always make it easy to develop a common understanding and agree on next steps.

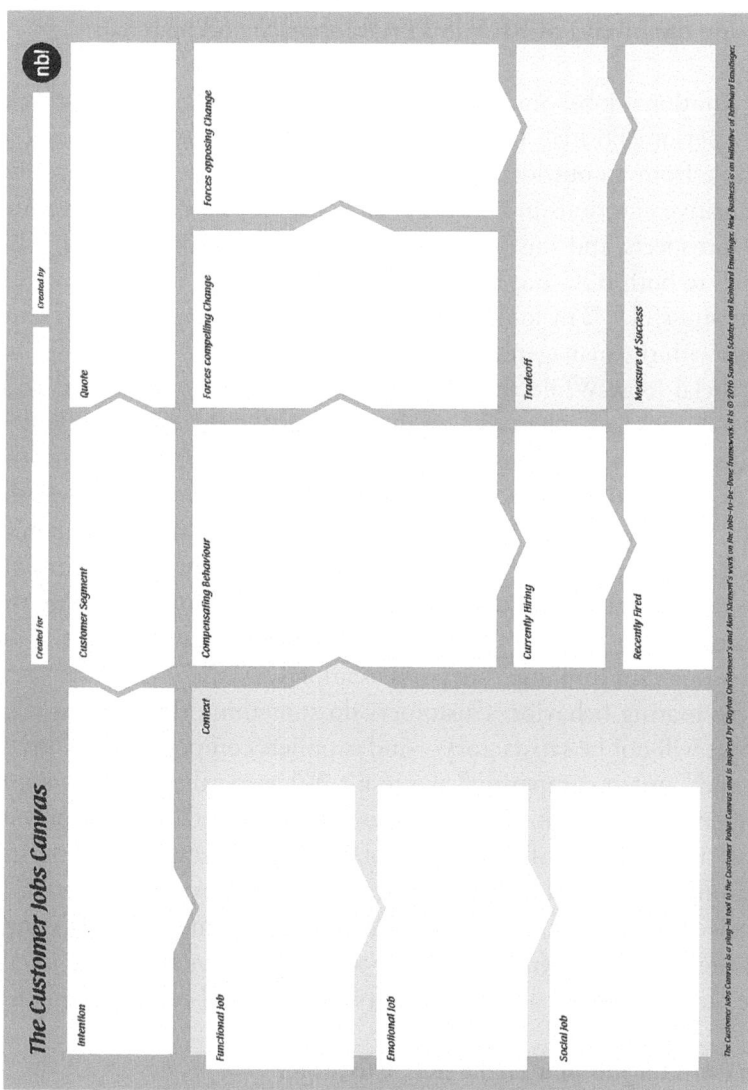

Fig. 2.12 Structure of the Customer Jobs Canvas

The authors therefore take the companies described in Sect. 1.4 and select the following three building blocks of HEDAKU's Customer Jobs Canvas and make them a little more tangible with the help of models built using the LEGO SERIOUS PLAY approach and materials:

- The emotional jobs: Similar to the customer journey in design thinking, a person's positive and negative emotions are considered as best as possible from an outsider's perspective. Looking at a person's positive or negative emotions in context is an essential part of understanding why prospects and customers buy, don't buy, or do nothing. This applies to both B2C and B2B. Good examples are "I find the environment stressful," "I'm looking forward to the meeting," or "I'm frustrated with the management."
- The social jobs: While the emotional jobs are solely concerned with how a person feels when solving the functional tasks, the focus here is on how others see that person. The important question here is how the person in question is perceived, or would like to be perceived, by others in his or her role in the organization—which may include family and friends. This could be customers, partners, competitors, important friends, suppliers, or social media. "I'm in control," "I'm the decision-maker (and the whole family knows it)," and "I want to be seen as forward thinking" are good examples.
- Compensating behavior: Customers do something that they at least suspect will not be satisfactory—and suppliers compete with an invisible and "'unfair competitor" as a result. Wherever there is evidence of compensating behavior by key customers or their fallback solutions, this is a clear signal of untapped potential. If customers are working hard on a solution that is mediocre in their context, an offer that is perceived as more useful will be all the more welcome. Real-life examples include "I concentrate on day-to-day business and don't plan," "We buy inferior but available quality," and "I send countless emails."

The Emotional Job of a HEDAKU Customer
The founder explains his most important customer segment—private dog owners with a good income and a keen interest in their pets—using the model as an example: "The model represents the emotional part of my

Fig. 2.13 The emotional job of a customer

customers' jobs as dog owners. The minifigure is deliberately understated in color, it doesn't push itself into the foreground and it's not loud. The headgear suggests that he is relaxed and somehow cool, and he is walking his dog without a lead. They understand each other without speaking. The figure is holding gold in his hand, which means that he is ready to spend money. He sees it as his task to ward off evil from his animal, which I have represented by the ghost behind the fence. The coffee pot and the chest with its contents symbolize that he makes sure that the animal gets enough food and that it is of excellent quality. The golden bowl filled with flowers symbolizes that my client takes special care to ensure that his dog has lots of fun and variety." Figure 2.13 shows the LEGO model described.

The Social Job of a HEDAKU Customer
The founder again describes the image of his most important customer and how he would probably like to be perceived by those around him: "This model shows the same customer as in the first model. His position and that

Fig. 2.14 The social job of a customer

of the dog have not changed much, and the coffee cup in his hand suggests that they are out and about in the morning. To the right of the customer are eyes watching him, which are actually uninteresting but harmless passers-by. Next to them is an 'empty' monster with a broom, a trowel and a megaphone – that's the pet owners who know everything better. However, a see-through fence keeps the eyes and the monster away from him without shielding him. On his left are friends, some approaching him, others just watching. The working day lies ahead of him, and money lies in the street as he walks through the window to his current tasks. He wants to be seen as someone who has everything under control and takes good care of his animal." Figure 2.14 shows the LEGO model described.

The Compensating Behavior of a HEDAKU Customer
The founder explains his third model by describing the compensating behavior of his most important customer segment as follows: "These are

potential customers who will probably never become customers. Both the client and his horse have now become skeletons, having starved to death halfway up the ladder. The goal is represented by the flowers at the top of the ladder, either it's too high or something is preventing the customer from reaching the flowers. This is what I mean by the actual low grey wall and the harmless snake in front of the ladder. With the model I mean that there are actually interesting customers for me, who might even be interested in my product, but they just can't get going. They just can't make up their minds, they browse here for ages, surf there for hours, but don't decide to buy or even try anything. For me it's not worth chasing them, the effort isn't worthwhile." Figure 2.15 shows the LEGO model described.

Fig. 2.15 The compensating behavior of a customer

2.4 Key Takeaways

When workshop participants think with their hands and three-dimensional objects, forgetting about time and place, they release creative energies and new perspectives that most adults don't even know they have. The concept of LEGO SERIOUS PLAY helps to recall and reactivate these skills. So, what are the concrete benefits?

The benefits for employees:

- Participants develop a shared understanding of an organization's current situation and possible realistic future scenarios.
- Their own contribution to the big picture is clearly visible to everyone around the table, and the contribution of others is better understood.
- Everyone's perspective on their own organization and its current and future fans, customers, partners, and competitors is broadened.

The benefits for managers:

- Newly gained insights can be quickly translated into comprehensible strategies that enable immediate concrete action.
- A shared understanding of the situation and the joint development of possible solutions increases everyone's willingness to implement them.
- Hierarchies, departmental boundaries, and silos can be playfully overcome, as everyone at the table has a voice that is heard and understood.

The benefits for founders and owners:

- Both the opportunities and challenges that an organization faces now and in the future are put on the table.
- The organization's vision and mission finally become clear, as does the potential contribution of all internal and external stakeholders.
- Personal intrinsic knowledge that has been buried becomes accessible, and good ideas can build on each other without the usual self-imposed limitations.

References

Csíkszentmihályi, Mihaly. 2010. *Flow - der Weg zum Glück*. Freiburg: Herder.
Ematinger, Reinhard, and Sandra Schulze. 2018. *Produkte und Services vom Kunden aus denken*. Wiesbaden: Springer Gabler.
Hahn, Kurt. 1930. Salemer Gesetze nach Kurt Hahn. www.kurt-hahn-stiftung.de/ueber-die-stiftung/kurt-hahn/. Accessed 1 June 2024.
Hammer, Michael, and Steven Stanton. 1995. *The reengineering revolution—A handbook*. New York: HarperCollins.
Kim, W. Chan, and Renée Mauborgne. 2005. *Blue ocean strategy - How to create uncontested market space and make the competition irrelevant*. Boston: Harvard Business School Press.

3

Target Definition in 3D

With this section, the authors invite you, after the first steps with LEGO SERIOUS PLAY, to apply this format to the formulation and communication of objectives. You can understand this format even better with the help of the four companies presented.

3.1 Problems and Solutions

Not even a visionary like Peter Drucker could have predicted with sufficient certainty the extent to which his Management by Objectives approach, proposed in the 1950s, would be adopted by organizations of all sizes and sectors. However, while a 2013 study by Mercer Global found that 95% of the 1000 organizations surveyed agreed individual objectives with their employees, a 2019 study published by the company comes to a different, thought-provoking conclusion. Although 83% of the 1100 HR professionals surveyed said that individual objectives are agreed with employees in their organizations, only 56% of these organizations agree objectives at a departmental level. According to the authors, this means that around half of these organizations are setting objectives in a vacuum, as employees' objectives are not linked to those of departments or even the company. As a result, it is difficult to recognize individuals' individual contributions to the organization's development (Mercer 2013, 2019).

In addition, the traditional approach of setting individual objectives only once a year and according to the well-known SMART criteria—specific, measurable, achievable, realistic, time-bound—is rarely challenged. The link to variable pay does not make it any easier to agree on truly ambitious targets.

The authors of the MIT Sloan article "With Goals, FAST Beats SMART" looked at the objective-setting processes of companies such as Google, Intel, and Anheuser-Busch (Sull and Sull 2018) and analyzed more than 500,000 objective definitions. In their article, they describe the four FAST principles that they believe underpin truly effective goal systems:

First principle—**f**requently discussed:

- Definition: Objectives should be discussed regularly to determine progress, plan resources, prioritize new initiatives, and create space for feedback.
- Benefit: Stakeholders focus on the most important activities, create binding guidelines for important decisions, and allow for quicker course corrections.

Second principle—**a**mbitious:

- Definition: As discussed in Sects. 2.1 and 2.3, the goals can be ambitious and challenging, but they must also be achievable with some effort.
- Benefit: Participants do not set their goals too low, as is usually the case with monetary incentives, but find ways to achieve high goals.

Third principle—specific:

- Definition: Objectives should be specific and clearly defined, as this is the only way to signal what outcome is expected, from whom, and what progress has been made so far.
- Benefit: Participants do not have to guess what is expected of them and can easily check what is working for them and others and where course corrections are needed.

Fourth principle—transparent:

- Definition: Objectives and progress should be transparent to everyone in the organization at all times, in order to see the link to the vision and create synergies.
- Benefit: In addition to understanding their own contribution to the organization's goals, people can also understand those of other teams and identify redundant activities.

In addition to medium and large organizations in various industries, these principles also support founders in defining their own objectives, which the authors describe in Sects. 1.4 and 3.4. In conjunction with the FAST Principles, the concept of Objectives and Key Results helps to link these short-term objectives to results and to make them verifiable.

3.2 Agenda at a Glance

As already mentioned in Sect. 2.2, the authors are primarily addressing you in your role as a facilitator or coach who supports clients in defining their objectives. If you want to use the concept of Objectives and Key Results with LEGO SERIOUS PLAY as a tool for yourself and your own ideas, the same procedure applies. In this case, you guide yourself through the process and document the results.

It is best to use one LEGO SERIOUS PLAY Starter Kit per person with order number 2000414 and one Identity and Landscape Kit with order number 2000430. For safe construction and storage, the authors recommend building on plates. The 8 × 16 plates with design number 92438 are ideal for small models, while the 16 × 16 plates with design number 91405 are perfect for larger models.

To create a safe environment in which relaxed building and explaining is possible, the following framework consisting of these seven points has proven to be useful:

- The process of building is more important than a particularly elaborate model. It is about creating a kind of three-dimensional metaphor as an answer to the question of goals.
- The result of the construction must be open, and as a facilitator you do not set any restrictions other than a time limit. Imagination should be given free rein.
- Make sure that you have undisturbed time and full concentration during the construction. Good models and stories are not created on the fly. Stop the process if there are distractions.
- If you or your client is unsure about what exactly to build, how much to build, and which bricks to use, just start building. Do not overthink the end result.
- Functionality is not important. As the story is told, the bricks that make up the model take on meaning for you and the others, even if the model is not perfect.
- If you are facilitating the process, ask "the model," not the person, if something is not clear to you. The story of the model is important, not the intention of the person.
- Everything that is built is explained. This also means that anything that is not being built at the moment has no place in the story about the model and is likely to be a distraction.

The core process described in Sect. 2.2 also provides a useful framework here and guides you through the next steps in defining your objectives:

- Step 1—Posing the question: The task is to build a picture of an objective for the next quarter from the available bricks. Examples of objectives from the three companies HEDAKU, BRNHLD, AVATAR, and VISUAL can be found in Sect. 1.4.

- Step 2—Build a model: Your client or you build models out of LEGO bricks in response to the first, second, and third objectives. Pictures of models made by HEDAKU, BRNHLD, AVATAR, and VISUAL can be found in Sect. 3.4.
- Step 3—Sharing the story: Your client presents his models and takes as much time as he wants. As facilitator, you listen attentively. Explanations of the models of HEDAKU, BRNHLD, AVATAR, and VISUAL can be found in Sect. 3.4.
- Step 4—Reflecting on the story: Together with you, your client reflects on his own story about the three models that represent his objectives. Your questions help them to find important details in the models and "translate" them into further thinking.

The authors recommend keeping the LEGO models until the current OKR cycle is completed. Make sure that the models are photographed from different angles in addition to the video recordings.

The information in Sect. 3.4 gives an idea of what a description might look like. The authors use the "Just Press Record" app for iOS and Android for documentation, as it automatically transcribes the spoken explanations of the LEGO models in a few seconds and provides at least a reasonably legible written form in addition to the audio recording.

3.3 Detailed Agenda (Tables 3.1 and 3.2)

Table 3.1 Overview on the detailed agenda

Goal	Joint definition of the Objectives and their Key Results for the next implementation cycle
Duration	1 day
Materials	• 1 starter kit per person
	• 1 identity and landscape kit
	• Plates 16 × 16, design number 91405, for Objectives
	• Plates 8 × 16, design number 92438, for Key Results
	• Connections for Key Results (e.g., strings)
Room	• Table for the participants
	• Table for LEGO materials
	• Tables for explaining and placing
	• Tables for the objectives and their Key Results
	• Tables for non-selected objectives
Participants	8

Table 3.2 Timeline of the detailed agenda

Start	Duration		Question
08:30	01:00	Introduction	Introduction to the workshop and the agenda
		Skills building	Tower
			First warm-up exercise; see Sect. 3.2
			Second warm-up exercise; see Sect. 3.2
			Third warm-up exercise; see Sect. 3.2
09:30	00:10	Objectives	If the participants are not familiar with the concept of Objectives and Key Results, it is necessary to introduce it here with examples. Focus on the Objectives part and please also note the specifics of Objectives (qualitative, inspiring, scheduled, executable)—See Sect. 2.1 "origin and background"
09:40	00:20		"You know the direction we want to take our organization (e.g.)"
			Build a model that represents a challenging but achievable objective for your team to achieve over the next 3 months. This objective should be realistic. It should challenge you as a team and require effort and commitment to achieve
			How you achieve the objective as a team is completely irrelevant. It's all about the objective itself. Make it as clear and specific as possible
10:00	00:20		Note: The models should be clear and specific. If this is not the case, the participants should concretize the models in a second round
10:20	00:30		Each participant now has a model of an Objective, usually with a rich history. They should now capture the essence of the model. Write it down in one sentence on a Post-It® note
			Remember the requirements from Sect. 2.1 "origin and background." Objectives should be qualitative, inspiring, scheduled, executable
			The history of the models is recorded and transcribed. The models are photographed in detail from all sides—The details are important
10:50	00:05		Participants are given three sticky dots per person and vote for each model. The aim is to choose three objectives per cycle. The authors recommend keeping the documentation of the other objectives and to point them out to the participants. The objectives developed can be referred to in a later cycle
10:55	00:10	Coffee break	

11:05	00:10	Key results for objective 1	If the participants are not familiar with the concept of Objectives and Key Results, it is necessary to introduce it here with examples. Focus on the Key Results part and please also note the specificities of Key Results (ground-breaking, measurable, achievable, results-oriented)—See Sect. 2.1 "origin and background"
11:15	00:20		"Imagine that <Objective 1> has been realised. Build two Key Results with which you can concretely measure that you have achieved this objective"
11:35	00:20		Note: The models representing the key results should be concrete, measurable, and feasible (see above). If this is not the case, the participants should concretize the models in a second round so that they meet the requirements of the key results
11:55	00:45	Lunch break	
12:40	00:50	Key results for objective 1	"Now look at the Key Results in front of you. Use links to show which Key Results are dependent on each other. Mark which is the dependent Key Result." Since the Key Results should be independent of each other, the dependent Key Results are placed on a separate table
13:30	00:05		Participants are given three sticky dots per person and use them to vote for the remaining models (the independent key outcomes). The aim is to choose three Key Results for Objective 1
13:35	00:05		The participants write down Objective 1 and the three corresponding key results in the following formula: We want to achieve <Objective 1> and we measure this with <Key Result 1> and <Key Result 2> and <Key Result 3>
13:40	00:05		
13:45	00:10	Coffee break	

(continued)

Table 3.2 (continued)

Start	Duration		Question
13:55	00:20	Key results for objective 2	"Imagine that <Objective 2> has been realised. Build two key results with which you can concretely measure that you have achieved the objective"
14:15	00:20		Note: The models representing the key results should be concrete, measurable, and feasible (see above). If this is not the case, the participants should concretize the models in a second round so that they meet the requirements of the key results
14:35	00:50		"Now look at the Key Results in front of you. Use links to show which Key Results are dependent on each other. Mark which is the dependent Key Result" Since the Key Results should be independent of each other, the dependent Key Results are placed in a separate table
15:25	00:05		Participants are given three sticky dots per person and use them to vote for the remaining models (the independent key outcomes). The aim is to choose three Key Results for Objective 2
15:30	00:05		The participants note Objective 2 and the three corresponding key results in the following formula: We want to achieve <Objective 2> and we measure this with <Key Result 1> and <Key Result 2> and <Key Result 3>
15:35	00:10	Coffee break	
15:45	00:05	Key results for objective 2	"Imagine that <Objective 3> has been realised. Build two key results with which you can concretely measure that you have achieved the objective"
15:50	00:20		Note: The models representing the key results should be concrete, measurable, and feasible (see above). If this is not the case, the participants should concretize the models in a second round so that they meet the requirements of the key results
16:10	00:20		"Now look at the Key Results in front of you. Use links to show which Key Results are dependent on each other. Mark which is the dependent Key Result." Since the Key Results should be independent of each other, the dependent Key Results are placed in a separate table
16:30	00:50		Participants are given three sticky dots per person and use them to vote for the remaining models (the independent key outcomes). The aim is to choose three Key Results for Objective 3
17:20	00:05		The participants note Objective 3 and the three corresponding key results in the following formula: We want to achieve <Objective 3> and we measure this with <Key Result 1> and <Key Result 2> and <Key Result 3>

3.4 Cases and Applications

The authors take up the examples of real Objective definitions from the companies HEDAKU, BRNHLD, AVATAR, and VISUAL presented in Sect. 1.4 and discuss the respective targets with the help of models built using the LEGO SERIOUS PLAY approach and materials.

As the companies and their application of the Objectives and Key Results are anonymized, the illustrations show only one of the three objectives in the form of a model from the most meaningful perspective. The models have been interpreted by their authors, who have smoothed the original tone to make them more readable without changing the meaning of the statements.

The Objective of HEDAKU
Of the three objectives (creating a solid organizational framework, preparing an exciting brand, designing a "likeable" product), the authors and the founder chose the third.

He explains the model as follows: "This represents my Objective—a 'likeable' product has been created: The minifigure representing me is very happy, toasts with a cup and has jets on his feet to show his special drive. The megaphone represents the next important activity, communicating my offer. The bowl closest to the figure is filled with flowers, symbolizing the obvious—the expected positive comments from future customers. The bowl further away, filled with coins and gold bars, represents the next but one step—the translation of social media likes into real life purchases. The crown, intentionally hung high, symbolizes the goals I've set for the next few quarters—happy customers who are happy to tell my story." Figure 3.1 shows the LEGO model described.

The Objective of BRNHLD
From the three objectives (we enjoy our topics, all topics generate good revenue, we are recognized), the authors chose the third objective in consultation with the consultant.

Fig. 3.1 The answer "A 'likeable' product is designed"

He explains his model as follows: "This picture shows my Objective 'We get noticed': The three minifigures represent enthusiastic customers, readers and consumers, perhaps even loyal fans. They look very different and can be entrepreneurs, company employees or even consultants, presenters and trainers. Some of them are on the move, like the one with the blue cap, while others have made themselves comfortable. That means they're taking the time to consume our content, maybe even to think about it, but they're not just casually clicking 'like' in passing, they're really engaging with it. I'm the all-white character, and that means it's not the person that's important, it's the content and the message. I approach the customers. There is an owl behind me, which symbolizes my claim. With the two weird ducks, I mean that it can also be fun, for my customers and for me." Figure 3.2 shows the LEGO model described.

3 Target Definition in 3D   63

Fig. 3.2 The answer "We are noticed"

The Objective of AVATAR

From the three objectives (an alternative supplier has been found, my marketing strategy has been designed, I am having fun with my customers), the owner has also chosen the third objective.

This is how he explains his model: "The model represents the goal 'I have fun with my customers': The cake represents my product, which I explain, and the flowers mean that I prepare a flower bed for the customers to move around in. From this togetherness something common can grow, an interest in each other. That's what this tree represents—the relationship with the customer, including the product sales, but above all a relationship that benefits both parties. The different heads represent the many customers from different sectors and also my ability to respond to their different needs. I have to be able to identify these needs, name them and tailor my communication to them. I don't sell a product. I'm selling the satisfaction of a need. If customers feel they have been

Fig. 3.3 The answer "I have fun with my customers"

listened to, they will buy my product." Figure 3.3 shows the LEGO model described.

The Objective of VISUAL
From the three objectives (I discover new business areas, my publications earn money, I take the next technological steps), the authors and the managing director have chosen the first Objective.

She explains her model as follows: "This work shows my objective 'I discover new fields of business': this little man is me, recognizable by my blonde hair and my big laugh—you can see that I really enjoy it. I'm holding a pair of binoculars and looking at the screen, at the new business areas. It shows a bit of magic sparkle and therefore a bit of poetry, but also

3   Target Definition in 3D   65

Fig. 3.4 The answer "I discover new business areas"

interlocking cogs that represent evolution. The flower represents development, and the other plant symbolizes growth. The two kings represent different clients. The boat has a propeller and with the momentum I am riding a wave and heading straight for the canvas. Here in the foreground, you can see a dog with a hot dog on its back, and maybe it and my comics have something to do with it. I'm also making money from it, as these coins show, because I've discovered these new areas." Figure 3.4 shows the LEGO model described.

3.5 The Takeaways

The combination of Objectives and Key Results with the activating approach of LEGO SERIOUS PLAY makes the sometimes-vague themes around one's own objectives tangible and achievable, from which results and activities can be more easily derived. What are the concrete benefits?

The benefits for employees:

- The individual contribution is more visible than when working with two dimensions and is also remembered for longer.
- Issues relating to personal and organizational goals, previously hidden between the lines, finally come to light.
- The 3D view of the "translation" of the corporate vision into concrete objectives invites others to join the discussion.

The benefits for managers:

- Focusing on the most important topics without distraction is "built into" LEGO SERIOUS PLAY.
- A complete picture of the whole team's point of view is created because everyone involved has a voice and is heard.
- A shared view of the Objectives increases the willingness of all those involved to make a real contribution to achieving them.

The benefits for founders and owners:

- Your own short-term Objectives and Key Results are more consciously perceived when they are manifested as a 3D image.
- Gaps and loose ends become clearer in the process of building and storytelling than when working in two dimensions.
- Realization with LEGO SERIOUS PLAY ensures that the Objectives are almost automatically always in view.

References

Mercer, ed. 2013. *2013 global performance management survey report.* New York: Mercer.

———, ed. 2019. Mercer's 2019 global performance management survey. www.imercer.com/uploads/common/HTML/LandingPages/AnalyticalHub/june2019-mercer-2019-global-performance-management-survey-executive-summary.pdf. Accessed 1 June 2024.

Sull, Donald, and Sull, Charles. 2018. With goals, FAST beats SMART. https://sloanreview.mit.edu/article/with-goals-fast-beats-smart/. Accessed 1 June 2024.

4

Retrospective in 3D

In this section, the authors invite you to apply this format to a retrospective after formulating objectives with the help of LEGO SERIOUS PLAY. The four companies discussed in Sects. 1.4 and 3.4 will help you to understand this better.

4.1 Problems and Solutions

Inviting a retrospective at the wrong time and in the wrong place often causes confusion in the team, as too many of these meetings are perceived as time-consuming and unhelpful in the environment of agile project management, scrum, and sprints.

Why is this the case? The authors suggest three reasons:

- There is a lack of real focus and real participation: The team discusses topics for which there is no room in this format. The tight time frame also means that the really important issues are not on the agenda. In addition, team members either stay away from the meeting or attend

© The Author(s), under exclusive license to Springer Nature Switzerland AG 2024
R. Ematinger et al., *Setting Goals with LEGO® SERIOUS PLAY®*, Business Guides on the Go, https://doi.org/10.1007/978-3-031-67857-8_4

but do not contribute their views on possible hurdles and problems that have arisen.
- Real insights are missing: The originally useful idea of time constraints gets in the way, especially when it comes to getting to the bottom of problems. The danger lies in collecting symptoms and trying to "solve" them superficially. Answers without a factual basis and agreement on actions without understanding the issues behind the symptoms are unlikely to lead to sustainable solutions.
- Real implementation is lacking: Even when there is consensus on the problems to be addressed, the proposed solutions are rarely concrete. Change can only begin when there is a shared understanding of the need and urgency, and when defined actions are implemented when maintaining the status quo is more uncomfortable than setting out for new and possibly uncertain shores.

The need to take a step back from the day-to-day, to pause and give yourself and each other time, is undeniable. A kind of helicopter perspective is needed to answer questions about what could be done better and how. This is precisely the purpose of a retrospective: a regular exchange that can take place "apart" from the measurement of results carried out in the reviews.

It also makes sense for founders and entrepreneurs working alone to take the aforementioned step back from the day-to-day business: issues of collaboration are not necessarily limited to one's own organization, but also include business partners such as suppliers and customers. The environment that cannot be directly influenced, such as the public, the press, bloggers, and analogue and digital influencers, should also be part of such a consideration, as should your own reaction to any trends that may be relevant to your own offering, changes in customer behavior, or potential competitors on the horizon.

Especially when there is little routine and a lot of new and unfamiliar things to process, it is worth answering these questions:

- What has happened in the last three months?
- What is my general mood?

- What did I do particularly well?
- What can I possibly do better?

The retrospective is a space to answer such questions without judgment, or at least to put them in concrete terms. Results are not so important—facts have their place in the review of Objectives and Key Results. The well-known advice on the "right" formats and locations from popular forums, articles, and books is not always useful. A review that takes place without a fixed agenda and away from the usual conference room atmosphere is likely to be more useful than the same plan every week or quarter.

The authors want to share these thoughts not only with medium and large organizations, but also with founders and entrepreneurs—and the facilitators and coaches who support them. The concept of Objectives and Key Results is not just about regularly setting objectives and reviewing results, but also about regularly taking time out to reflect on your own work. Examples of this can be found in Sect. 4.3.

4.2 Agenda at a Glance

As in Sects. 2.2 and 3.2, the authors are primarily addressing you in your role as a facilitator or coach helping clients to define their goals. If you want to use the concept of Objectives and Key Results with LEGO SERIOUS PLAY as a tool for yourself and your own ideas, the same procedure applies. In this case, you guide yourself through the process and document the results.

The bricks and plates suggested in Sect. 3.2 are ideal for this activity, and the framework discussed in the same section is also helpful.

The core process described above also provides a useful framework here and guides you through the next steps in defining objectives:

- Step 1—Posing the question: The challenge is to answer a question from the available bricks that corresponds to your personal view of the quarter that is coming to an end and your own assessment of it. Examples of questions can be found in Sect. 4.4.

- Step 2—Build a model: Your client or you build your models out of LEGO bricks in response to the formulated question within a given time frame. Pictures of models from HEDAKU, BRNHLD, and AVATAR can be found in the following chapter.
- Step 3—Sharing the story: Your client introduces his model and takes as much time as they want. As the facilitator, you listen attentively again. Explanations of the HEDAKU, BRNHLD, AVATAR, and VISUAL models can also be found in Sect. 4.4.
- Step 4—Reflecting on the story: Together with you, your client reflects on their own story about the model that represents their view in the rear-view mirror. Your questions help to find and formulate important and previously unspoken details in the model.

Again, the authors recommend keeping the LEGO model until the current period of objective setting and review is complete. Make sure that it is also photographed from a number of different angles.

4.3 Detailed Agenda (Tables 4.1 and 4.2)

Table 4.1 Overview on the detailed agenda

Goal	Evaluating the effectiveness and efficiency of specific Objectives and Key Results within a review. Retrospective of the OKR process to make it even more effective for the team
Duration	1 day
Materials	• Starter kits • Identity and landscape kits
Room	• Table for the participants • Table for LEGO materials • Tables for explaining and placing • Tables for reviewing the Objectives and their Key Results • Tables for reviewing the OKR process
Participants	8

Table 4.2 Timeline of the detailed agenda

Start	Duration		Question
08:30	01:00	Introduction	Introduction to the workshop and the agenda
		Skills building	Tower
09:30	00:15		First warm-up exercise; see Sect. 3.2
09:45	00:05		Second warm-up exercise; see Sect. 3.2
			Third warm-up exercise; see Sect. 3.2
		Coffee break	
		Review of Objective 1	Review of Objective 1 with the reminder: We want to achieve <Objective 1> and we measure this with <Key Result 1> and <Key Result 2> and <Key Result 3>.
09:50	00:20		What was good about realizing the Key Results of Objective 1? One model per aspect
10:10	00:20		What did not go well in the realization of the Key Results of Objective 1? One model per aspect
10:30	00:20		Based on what you have gathered: • What do you take with you? • What are your lessons learnt?
10:50	00:20		Documentation: Video and Post-Its®
11:10	00:05	Review of Objective 2	Review of Objective 2 with the reminder: We want to achieve <Objective 2> and we measure this with <Key Result 1> and <Key Result 2> and <Key Result 3>.
11:15	00:20		What was good about realizing the Key Results of Objective 2? One model per aspect
11:35	00:20		What did not go well in the realization of the Key Results of Objective 2? One model per aspect
11:55	00:20		Based on what you have gathered: • What do you take with you? • What are your lessons learnt?
12:15	00:20		Documentation: Video and Post-Its®

(continued)

Table 4.2 (continued)

Start	Duration		Question
12:35	00:45	Lunch break	
13:20	00:05	Review of Objective 3	Review of Objective 3 with the reminder: We want to achieve <Objective 3> and we measure this with <Key Result 1> and <Key Result 2> and <Key Result 3>.
13:25	00:20		What was good about realizing the Key Results of Objective 3? One model per aspect
13:45	00:20		What did not go well in the realization of the Key Results of Objective 3? One model per aspect
14:05	00:20		Based on what you have gathered: • What do you take with you? • What are your lessons learnt? Documentation: Video and Post-Its®
14:25	00:20	Coffee break	
14:45	00:10	Retrospective of the OKR process	Review of the entire OKR process
14:55	00:05		How did I feel about the OKR process in the last period? What was really good from planning to review? One model per aspect
15:00	00:20		
15:20	00:20		How did I feel about the OKR process in the last period? What was not good from planning to review? One model per aspect
15:40	00:20		Based on what you have gathered: • What do you take away? • What can be improved in the process? • What are your lessons learnt?
16:00	00:20		Documentation: Video and Post-Its®

4.4 Cases and Applications

The authors revisit the examples of the companies HEDAKU, BRNHLD, AVATAR, and VISUAL discussed in Sects. 1.4 and 3.4 and present the results of the retrospective. This first round of end-of-quarter review is intended to answer one of the following questions using the three-dimensional models:

- Does the OKR approach help me, or does it just get in the way?
- What did I notice during the process?
- How did we feel about working together?
- What changes are particularly noticeable?
- Were the agreed goals ambitious enough?
- Were the Key Results really meaningful?
- What is better "after" than "before"?
- What did I learn today that was totally new?
- What can I take away for the next round?
- What can we start with tomorrow?

The illustrations show the answer in the form of a model from the most meaningful point of view. Once again, the models were personally interpreted by their builders, with the authors smoothing out the original sound a little.

The Retrospective of HEDAKU
The founder asked himself the question "What is 'after' better than 'before'?" and answered it.

He explains his LEGO model like this: "The minifigure on the yellow platform represents me. The flower on my head represents the many good ideas I'm trying to realize, and the broom represents the work that lies ahead. I am in a good mood and the position of the figure's legs shows that I am making progress. Skeletons are moving on the red platform, reaching out to me with outstretched arms. I am referring to the many objects that distract me. The distractions look cool – hence the upturned red caps – and are, unfortunately, mostly exciting. I'm not directly in their field of vision either, the skeletons don't have me directly in their sights. They can only reach me via a small bridge with an eye on it, thanks

Fig. 4.1 The answer to the question of "before" and "after"

to my agreement with myself. The eye represents a kind of OKR alertness that ensures that the distractions are detected in time before they cross the bridge." Figure 4.1 shows the LEGO model described.

The Retrospective of BRNHLD
The consultant has answered the question about a particularly noticeable change and explains his model as follows: "The ghost and its dead horse are no longer a threat—they symbolize the many issues that could be tackled but are in fact more of a burden than an opportunity. They look cute at first glance, just like the friendly ghost, but they ensure that our own and others' perceptions are blurred rather than clear and unambiguous. The robot has also made itself comfortable and is sitting idly by. It stands for all sorts of technical things that are not my core competence and probably never will be. I'm on the ladder, taking the first steps towards a clear focus. The red teapot signals that I am relaxed. The green rope connects me to reality. It is not meant to protect me, but rather to ground me and ensure that the future topic is not far from the reality of my target groups." Figure 4.2 shows the LEGO model described.

Fig. 4.2 The answer to the question about the most noticeable change

The Retrospective of AVATAR

The owner has answered the question about the benefits of the OKR process and explains his model as follows: "The fact that I set myself these objectives three months ago and that I had them in writing – concretized and condensed into short sentences – is like a picture in my head. It's not something I have to read over and over again or stick on the wall. I can remember the objectives; they are in my head. This has made the orientation and the pursuit very concrete. There are few goals, very specific, precise and very short. The skeletons that surround me represent the fact that I have got to the heart of the matter in the customer contract, to the essentials, so to speak. In this picture I am standing on a net: In three months, I have managed to build a network and connect customers. They talk to each other on the phone and give each other feedback. I've done that in three months." Figure 4.3 shows the LEGO model described.

Fig. 4.3 The answer to the question about the benefits of the process

The Retrospective of VISUAL

The Managing Director answered the question, with the OKR approach helping her in particular, and explains her model as follows: "During the process, I found that defining intermediate steps helped me enormously. The picture shows three steps we worked out. This allowed me to move from one task to the next, one step at a time. This took away my fear of having too many tasks at once and losing track of what needed to be done. That's what this spirit on the bridge represents. The lady, that's me, has just reached the second step and is holding a clipboard – that's the to-do list. The third step, at the very end, shows that it was really worth it. The little man is the OKR champion who really knows and has experience of the topic. This is symbolized by the hat – the consultant is wearing the hat, so to speak. The plant at the bottom of the stairs symbolizes my growth." Figure 4.4 shows the LEGO model described.

Fig. 4.4 The answer to the question for support

4.5 The Takeaways

The LEGO models make it easier to understand what happened in the last quarter, what went well and what went less well, and what lessons can be learned for the coming months. What are the concrete benefits?

The benefits for employees:

- One's own position becomes clearer than when working with two dimensions and is remembered for longer.
- Any misunderstandings and unclear responsibilities in the processes are brought to the table.
- The 3D view of the past quarter's collaboration invites others to contribute to the dialogue.

The benefits for managers:

- Focusing on the most important issues without distraction is built into LEGO SERIOUS PLAY.
- Building and storytelling builds team spirit because everyone has a voice and is heard.
- A shared view of the current mood increases the willingness of others to contribute to change.

The benefits for founders and owners:

- One's own history and possible future is more consciously perceived when it is manifested as a 3D image.
- Gaps and loose ends become more apparent as you build and tell the story, compared to working in two dimensions.
- The playful approach of LEGO SERIOUS PLAY ensures that the clear focus on improvement is sustainable.

4.6 Instead of a Summary

With this contribution, the authors want to help you take your first steps with the meaningful combination of Objectives and Key Results and LEGO SERIOUS PLAY.

Why do we do this?

- Because we believe that Objectives and Key Results create a clear focus for a manageable period of time and build a bridge from the corporate vision to the necessary activities.
- Because we believe that LEGO SERIOUS PLAY makes previously vague issues tangible and helps you to express your own point of view and to understand yourself and others better.
- Because we believe that the intelligent combination of these approaches helps to bring their objectives, and the questions and answers that go with them, to the table and to create a shared vision.

There is no Right or Wrong. Just helpful. Use what works for you, modify what doesn't seem right, and get started. "Leg godt!"—play well!

What You Can Take Away from this *Business Guide on the Go*

- Suggestions for a process that makes working with Objectives and Key Results tangible and brings important issues to the table.
- Real and up-to-date examples to help you "translate" the approach into your reality and multiply it.
- Useful tips in the "What to take away" chapters to help you transfer them to your organization.

The manufacturer's authorised representative in the EU is Springer Nature Customer Service Centre GmbH, Europaplatz 3, 69115 Heidelberg, Germany. If you have any concerns regarding our products, please contact ProductSafety@springernature.com

Printed and bound by CPI Group (UK) Ltd, Croydon, CR0 4YY

26/03/2026

02078916-0001